DEALEY

THE FRONT DOOR OF DALLAS

PLAZA

DEALEY PLAZA
The Front Door of Dallas

Arlinda Abbott

Dallas, Texas
2003

Published by
The Sixth Floor Museum at Dealey Plaza
411 Elm Street, Suite 120
Dallas, Texas 75202-3301
214 747-6660

Printed by Buchanan Visual Communications, Dallas, Texas

Designed by Jonathan Ingram, i.design, www.ingramdesign.com, Dallas, Texas

Photographs of artifacts on pages 17, 20, 22-23, 28-29, 30, 33, 40, 49 by Tom Jenkins, Dallas, Texas

This publication complements the exhibition
Dealey Plaza: The Front Door of Dallas
The Sixth Floor Museum at Dealey Plaza
November 2002-November 2003

ISBN 0-9648131-7-3

Endsheet: The statue of G.B. Dealey was unveiled and
dedicated in Dealey Plaza on November 14, 1949. Courtesy Dallas Historical Society

Opposite: Taken in 2001, this aerial photograph provides a contemporary view
of Dealey Plaza. Courtesy MESA Design Group

This publication was made possible in part by a grant from

Long before November 22, 1963, the Dealey Plaza site was an important Dallas landmark. It was at this location in 1841 that John Neely Bryan founded what would become the city of Dallas. Our first government buildings were located here. It marked the location of important community gatherings and was the crossroads for the region's transportation—rail, street, and the Trinity River. ★ Completed in 1941, Dealey Plaza became our community's gateway facing westward toward our sister city—and rival—Fort Worth. Travelers coming from the west would pass under the railroad's triple underpass and emerge into a green transit park with beautiful Art Deco-style structures—an ambitious entry for an ambitious city. ★ So important was this location to the founding and development of Dallas that we commemorate some of our leading citizens at this site. The Plaza was named for George Bannerman Dealey, a Dallas legend and the publisher of *The Dallas Morning News*. The Bryan Colonnade on the north side of the Plaza was named in honor of Dallas founder John Neely Bryan, while the Cockrell Colonnade, named for city entrepreneurs Alexander and Sarah Cockrell, is located on the south side.

With such a rich history, it is all the more ironic that in November 1963, the event

that would forever scar and transform our city took place in Dealey Plaza. President

Kennedy's motorcade had been planned for weeks, with the parade route printed in both

Dallas newspapers. The crowds that welcomed President and Mrs. Kennedy to Dallas

that day were tremendous, as captured by the photographs and films taken at Love

Field and throughout downtown. An estimated 100,000 people lined the motorcade

route. ★ Approaching Dealey Plaza on Main Street, the presidential motorcade made a

right-hand turn north onto Houston and then a left-hand "hairpin" turn onto Elm Street

in order to access the freeway going north. There, in the shadow of the Texas School

Book Depository, our city was forever changed. ★ From battlefields to sites of natural

disasters, our country is abundant with places of pain and loss. These sites through

time are transformed into hallowed ground as we mark our nation's history. In that

respect, Dealey Plaza is identified most importantly by the assassination of President

John F. Kennedy. Nevertheless, it holds a great history of our community. For within its

confines, the spirit of Dallas was truly born.

Jeff West, *Executive Director*
The Sixth Floor Museum at Dealey Plaza

*...there was the rifle.
I could see the rifle...
being drawn in the
window...*

BOB JACKSON, former *Dallas Times Herald* photographer,
Oral History Project, The Sixth Floor Museum at Dealey Plaza,
November 22, 1993

Commemorative postcards
were available soon after the
Kennedy assassination. The
Sixth Floor Museum at Dealey Plaza

Sniper's Perch

Warehouse Building

Texas School Book Depository

Records Building

County Jail

Entrance to County
Jail Where Oswald Was
to Have Been Moved

MOTORCADE ROUTE

First Shot Hits Mr.
Kennedy in Back

Second Shot Wounds
Governor Connally

Third Shot Strikes Mr.
Kennedy in The Head

Elm. St.

Dealey Plaza

Assassination Scene
PRESIDENT JOHN FITZGERALD KENNEDY

Railroad Overpass

Shots were fired from the sixth-floor corner window of the Texas School Book Depository. Tom Dillard Collection/The Sixth Floor Museum at Dealey Plaza

Kennedy Slain in Dallas

On his visit to Dallas on November 22, 1963, President John F. Kennedy rode in a motorcade through Dealey Plaza, a three-acre vehicular park, on his way to the Dallas Trade Mart. In the presidential car with Kennedy were his wife Jacqueline, Texas Governor John Connally, and his wife Nellie. Hundreds of well-wishers were scattered throughout the Plaza. Nellie Connally's last words to Kennedy, "Mr. President, you can't say Dallas doesn't love you!" reflected the sentiment of the crowd. Suddenly, at 12:30 p.m., after the motorcade turned from Houston Street onto Elm Street, shots were fired, killing President Kennedy and wounding Governor Connally. Bob Jackson, a *Dallas Times Herald* photographer, was in a press car in the motorcade, eight cars behind the President. After he heard a third shot, Jackson looked up and spotted a rifle at a sixth-floor corner window in the Texas School Book Depository building.

This frame from the Robert Hughes home movie shows the Kennedys on Houston Street. Robert J.E. Hughes Collection/The Sixth Floor Museum at Dealey Plaza

This never-before-published photograph taken by Jay Skaggs shows President Kennedy's car immediately after it turned onto Houston Street and approached the Texas School Book Depository. Jay Skaggs Collection/The Sixth Floor Museum at Dealey Plaza

The motorcade crept slowly down Elm Street before the fatal shot. Phil Willis Collection/The Sixth Floor Museum at Dealey Plaza

Frame 230 in the Abraham Zapruder film of the assassination captured President Kennedy reacting to the first shot that struck him. Zapruder Collection/The Sixth Floor Museum at Dealey Plaza

Cradle and Grave

The land now known as Dealey Plaza was the birthplace of the city and county of Dallas founded by John Neely Bryan in the 1840s. It was also the site of Dallas' ultimate city planning solution—a vehicular park and a triple underpass. Built in the 1930s and 1940s during the fervor of the Texas Centennial and President Roosevelt's New Deal, these improvement projects were spearheaded by Dallas civic leader George Bannerman Dealey.

Hailed as "The Front Door of Dallas," Dealey Plaza served as the major gateway to the western edge of downtown and, equally important, as a symbol of the city's proud history. In 1963, the focus changed when President Kennedy was slain in the heart of the Plaza. Instantly, Dealey Plaza became an internationally recognized murder site.

After the assassination, Dealey Plaza presented Dallas with the controversy of how to address a place that served as both "cradle" and "grave"—a historic setting where Dallas was born and an American president died.

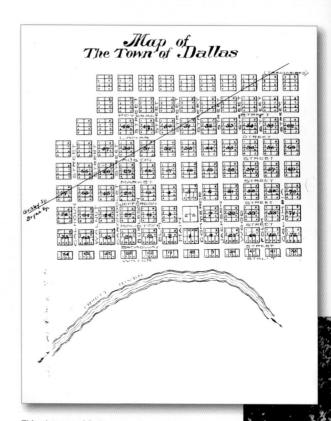

This plat map of Dallas was drawn in 1850, nine years after Bryan established the town. Courthouse Square is indicated by the scales of justice. Courtesy Dallas Historical Society

All weekend after the assassination, shocked and grieving Dallasites brought flowers and apologies to Dealey Plaza in memory of the slain President. Robert Russell Collection/The Sixth Floor Museum at Dealey Plaza

*...now you see people really being given an opportunity to come to this strange killing ground
out here and see with their own eyes...what happened.*

And that's the oddity of this place.
That it seems so banal...

*the concrete pergola from a WPA project, the curve downhill toward the freeway,
the railroad overpass, the Depository building...all of these totally banal city structures...
gain a kind of symbolic significance.*

JOSIAH THOMPSON, Kennedy assassination researcher and
author of *Six Seconds in Dallas*, Oral History Project,
The Sixth Floor Museum at Dealey Plaza, November 21, 1998

Dallas is Born

We had heard a great deal about the Three Forks of the Trinity and the town of Dallas...
We heard of it often, yes, the place, but the town where was it?

Two small log cabins...a shelter made of four sticks
for a smith shop, a garden fenced in with brush...

This was the town of Dallas and two families, ten or twelve souls were its population...
One deep, narrow and crooked channel was all we could see of the far famed Trinity River.

JOHN B. BILLINGSLEY, visitor from Missouri,
recorded in his journal in 1844

John Neely Bryan, founder of Dallas, and
Margaret Beeman were married in 1843.
Courtesy Texas/Dallas History and Archives
Division, Dallas Public Library

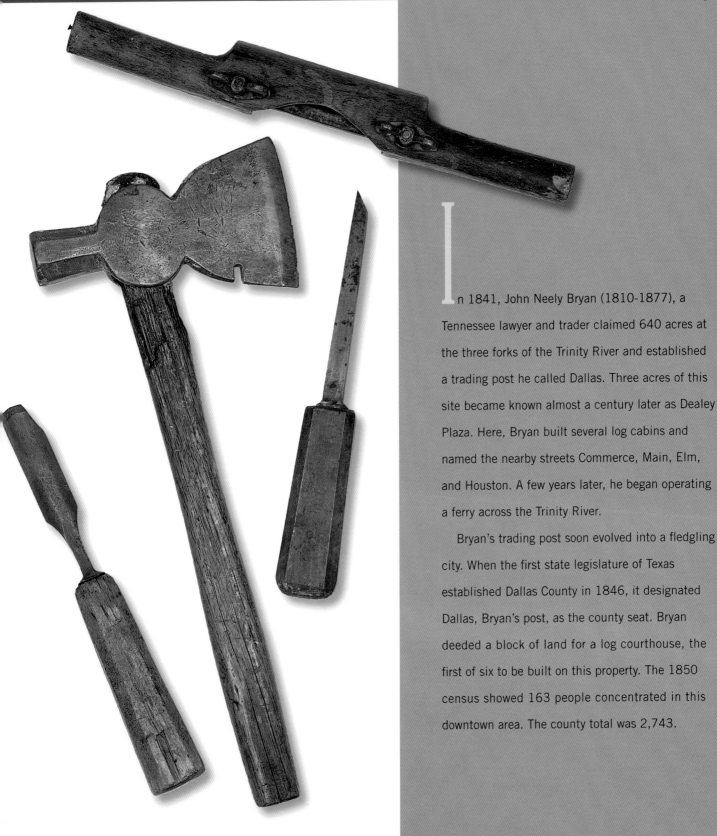

In 1841, John Neely Bryan (1810-1877), a Tennessee lawyer and trader claimed 640 acres at the three forks of the Trinity River and established a trading post he called Dallas. Three acres of this site became known almost a century later as Dealey Plaza. Here, Bryan built several log cabins and named the nearby streets Commerce, Main, Elm, and Houston. A few years later, he began operating a ferry across the Trinity River.

Bryan's trading post soon evolved into a fledgling city. When the first state legislature of Texas established Dallas County in 1846, it designated Dallas, Bryan's post, as the county seat. Bryan deeded a block of land for a log courthouse, the first of six to be built on this property. The 1850 census showed 163 people concentrated in this downtown area. The county total was 2,743.

These building tools—spoke shave, carpenter's axe, mortising chisel, and carving gouge—were used by La Reunion settlers prior to the Civil War. La Reunion, a short-lived French Utopian community, was located three miles southwest of Bryan's post. These tools were probably similar to those used by Bryan's colonists. *Courtesy Dallas Historical Society*

Accessibility to Dallas increased after business leader Alexander Cockrell engineered the first bridge across the Trinity River in 1858, and his enterprising wife Sarah opened an iron bridge after his death in 1872. A year later, the Texas & Pacific Railway laid its first tracks. By 1880, the county population jumped to over 33,000—it had increased more than twelve times in 30 years. Growth and expansion continued to be a priority in Dallas, and its citizens wanted a courthouse that would reflect the strength, elegance, and style of the city. In 1891, construction began on the blue granite and red Pecos sandstone building designed by architect Maximilian A. Orlopp. Completed in the early 1890s, "Old Red"—the sixth and last courthouse to be erected on the property donated by Bryan—became the centerpiece of the bustling city.

Stimulated by all this building activity, the Southern Rock Island Plow Company constructed a five-story warehouse to display and sell farm implements in 1898. After it was destroyed by fire, the company built a seven-story masonry structure in its place in 1901. Sixty years later, after housing several businesses, this building became known as the Texas School Book Depository. As other warehouses and government buildings were erected and railroad companies laid tracks, business in the downtown area prospered.

Successfully managing her husband's business interests after his death, Sarah Cockrell became one of Dallas' leading entrepreneurs. The City Directory listed her occupation as "capitalist." Courtesy Dallas Historical Society

Sarah Cockrell built this iron toll bridge in 1872. Courtesy Texas/Dallas History and Archives Division, Dallas Public Library

Dallas is to be grinned at no longer as a one horse town.

It has put away its petticoats and donned a new pair of 'britches' with pockets and a cigar in its mouth and is no longer a little boy...

**JOHN MILTON MCCOY, Dallas settler in a letter
to his parents in Illinois, July 7, 1872**

Business stationery depicts the Southern Rock Island Plow Company that was built in 1901. This building later became the Texas School Book Depository, where on November 22, 1963, shots were fired from a sixth-floor corner window at President Kennedy. *Courtesy Jeff Dunn*

Main Street in downtown Dallas was bustling at the turn of the 20th century. *Courtesy Dallas Historical Society*

19

When and by whom was Dallas named and settled? I ask.
And leading citizens are unable to answer me.

A Chicago editor to *The Dallas Morning News*, March 21, 1920

Was George Mifflin Dallas the "friend" for whom Bryan named his post? Lithograph by Currier & Ives. Courtesy Dallas County

GEORGE M. DALLAS.
THE PEOPLE'S CANDIDATE FOR
Vice President of the United States.
Lith. & Pub by N Currier 2 Spruce St N.Y.

Who was Dallas?

There has been much disagreement over the origin of the city's name—Dallas. Settler Frank M. Cockrell recalled founder John Neely Bryan claiming, "The town was named for my friend Dallas." But who was Dallas? Most people think Bryan named the place for George Mifflin Dallas, a Philadelphia lawyer and diplomat who was elected Vice President of the United States under James K. Polk in 1844. Historian L.W. Kemp disagreed. Kemp found newspaper reports that showed Dallas was named before November 22, 1843. At that time, Kemp reasoned, George Mifflin Dallas was practicing law in Philadelphia and it was doubtful Bryan had ever heard

A few other sources suggest

— the city was named for George Mifflin Dallas' brother, Alexander James Dallas, a naval captain who fought pirates in the West Indies after 1812;

— when Bryan was courting Margaret Beeman, he accepted her father's proposal that the settlement be called Dallas in exchange for his daughter's hand in marriage; and

— the wife of Captain Mabel Gilbert won a town lot at the northeast corner of Commerce and Houston Streets for suggesting the name Dallas.

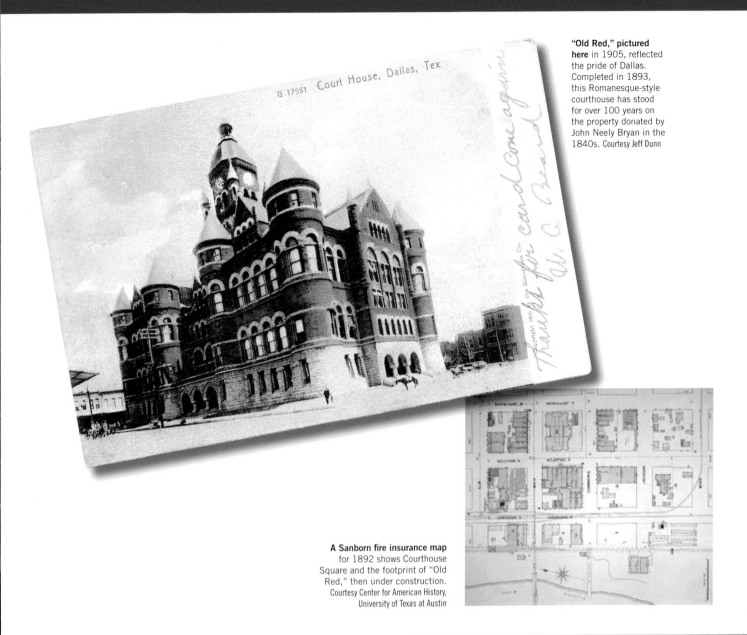

G 17551 Court House, Dallas, Tex.

A Sanborn fire insurance map for 1892 shows Courthouse Square and the footprint of "Old Red," then under construction. Courtesy Center for American History, University of Texas at Austin

Courthouse Square

Until the 1960s, the seat of Dallas County government had always been located on a parcel of land John Neely Bryan donated to the county. Before "Old Red" was built in the early 1890s, five ill-fated courthouses stood on this property bound by Main, Commerce, Houston, and Record Streets.

The first courthouse was a log cabin, 10 x 10 feet, with one door, one window, and a floor made of split logs, hewn smooth on one side. Standing only two years, fire destroyed it in 1848. A second larger log cabin, poorly built in 1850, was dismantled in 1857 to construct a brick courthouse. In October 1871, construction began on Dallas' fourth courthouse. Built from Dallas County limestone at a cost

of nearly $100,000, this courthouse was then considered the finest and most substantial building in the state. Unfortunately, it partially burned in 1880. James Flanders completed the fifth Dallas County courthouse in 1881. The French-inspired, Second Empire-style limestone edifice was believed to be the first fireproof structure in the city. Ironically, it burned down nine years later in August 1890.

Finally, in 1893 and at a cost of over $300,000, the sixth and longest-standing courthouse was completed and is fondly known today as "Old Red."

21

Champions of Dallas City Planning

G.B. Dealey of Dallas, Texas, has done more for city planning than any other individual in the United States.

GEORGE E. KESSLER, nationally known city planner, to a meeting of city planners in Kansas City, 1919

G.B. Dealey is shown here in the late 1930s printing the "Radio Edition" of *The Dallas Morning News* with an early Facsimile-receiver. Courtesy Texas/Dallas History and Archives Division, Dallas Public Library

This portable pen holder with ink well was used by G.B. Dealey in the 1930s. Courtesy Dallas Historical Society

Houston Street, looking north from Young Street, was overcrowded during the early 1900s. Courtesy Texas/Dallas History and Archives Division, Dallas Public Library

George Bannerman Dealey

In the early 20th century, Dallas was choking to death commercially. As architects built in the downtown district, citizens became concerned with the placement of the river, the rails, and the roads. Dallas was not equipped to accommodate the unprecedented growth. The city needed a plan.

It all began one evening in 1902. While George Bannerman Dealey (1859-1946), then vice president and general manager of *The Dallas Morning News*, stood on the Commerce Street Bridge, he was seized by an inspiration:

I was immediately possessed with the thought that vacant land in the bottom, which everyone considered worthless, would some day be available [for use]. I wanted some of that land... I closed the deal on borrowed money...and when I went home, I told my wife that it meant some day real wealth would come out of it.

Many years later, G.B. Dealey gave parcels of this land to the city and county to develop the triple underpass.

G.B. Dealey became a champion of city planning. He was armed with the notion that he could tame the Trinity River, which flowed west of downtown, by means of engineering and ingenuity. Even the 1908 flood did not discourage him. Determined to improve access to the city and control floodwaters, he garnered the support of local business leaders, city officials, and the Chamber of Commerce to form the Dallas City Plan and Improvement League.

For 50 years, G.B. Dealey frequented the Fretz Barber Shop, a prosperous Dallas establishment. Barber shops once served as headquarters to politicians and business leaders. It was a mark of distinction to have a personal shaving mug, like this one that belonged to G.B. Dealey, in the barber's case. Courtesy Dallas Historical Society

The Trinity River was shown navigable here shortly before the massive 1908 flood. Courtesy Jeff Dunn

At the Head of Navigation Dallas. Texas.

Trinity Crossings Wrecked by 1908 Flood

On May 25, 1908, the Trinity River, swollen by many days of heavy rain, became a rushing torrent that peaked at a height of 52 feet and spanned a width of one and a half miles. This major flood—the worst in Dallas' collective memory—left at least five people dead, 4,000 homeless, and property damage estimated at $2.5 million. All of west Dallas was under water; the entire city was devastated.

Bridge, Dallas, Texas.

The Trinity River flowed
at a normal level
beneath the Commerce
Street Bridge in this
card postmarked 1910.
Courtesy Jeff Dunn

Spectators viewed the Trinity River at its height
from the Commerce Street Bridge in 1908.
The Sixth Floor Museum at Dealey Plaza

Dallas' Great Improvement Project

In 1910, the city hired St Louis and Kansas City landscape architect and city planner, George E. Kessler (1862-1923), to prepare a master plan for Dallas. Masterminded by Kessler, the Improvement League assessed the city's needs. "The Trinity River project is the biggest problem you have in Dallas," Kessler pointed out. His plan for recovery included construction of 25 miles of 30-foot high levees. He also recommended a belt railway around the city, a union depot, joint freight yards, and the "absolute elimination of railway tracks on Pacific Avenue." The tracks hampered retail business and limited growth to the north.

Progress was slow. In 1916, Union Station opened, and in 1921, the last train passed on Pacific Avenue. The tracks were re-routed to the outskirts of town.

It was not until 1928, five years after Kessler's death, that construction of the Trinity levees got underway. G.B. Dealey was the honored speaker at the ground-breaking ceremony. The project employed an average of 1,000 men at a time. As many as 15 huge dragline machines worked 24 hours a day. The men and machines moved 21 million cubic yards of dirt to relocate the river one-half mile west into the middle of the flood plain and to build up the levees. This massive engineering project laid the groundwork for the construction of Dealey Plaza.

George E. Kessler gained recognition as a city planner through his park and boulevard work for Kansas City in 1893. He came to Texas to provide plans to many cities including Dallas, Fort Worth, El Paso, Sherman, and Wichita Falls. Courtesy Kansas City, Missouri, Board of Parks and Recreation Commissioners

Mr. Kessler made probably the greatest single contribution

*to the future welfare of Dallas that has been made...
since John Neely Bryan built his little log cabin
on the east bank of the Trinity.*

JUSTIN FORD KIMBALL, Dallas education official, 1954

The Trinity River levee project employed an average of 1,000 men at a time. Courtesy DeGolyer Library, Southern Methodist University, Dallas, Texas

Huge dragline machines worked around the clock to move dirt for the levees. Courtesy DeGolyer Library, Southern Methodist University, Dallas, Texas

TERMINAL STATION, DALLAS, TEXAS.

Designed by Chicago architect Jarvis Hunt and completed in 1916, Union Station provided passenger facilities for all of the nine railroads entering Dallas. Before that time there had been five separate stations in Dallas which added to the agitation and congestion in the city. Courtesy Jeff Dunn

Before levees were constructed, the Trinity River was thought to be untamable. Courtesy Texas/Dallas History and Archives Division, Dallas Public Library

The white lines indicated the relocated and straightened, four-mile downtown section of the Trinity River. Courtesy Texas/Dallas History and Archives Division, Dallas Public Library

Kessler's *A City Plan for Dallas,* published in 1912, spelled out the improvements necessary for planned growth. Kessler expanded the original plan in 1919 and 1920 to address the changing conditions and needs of the rapidly growing community. Courtesy Dallas Historical Society

Kessler's Dallas City Plan

Until the turn of the 20th century—many cities—like Dallas, developed haphazardly, without any attempt at planned growth. About 1893, city planning as a recognized profession evolved from park development and landscape architecture.

Kessler emerged in 1893 as a city planner through his park boulevard plan for Kansas City. G.B. Dealey had known Kessler since his work on the State Fair of Texas in 1904 and supported his selection. Kessler's *A City Plan for Dallas,* developed during 1911 and published in 1912, first addressed the Trinity River problems. He emphasized the need to provide flood protection for the entire city and specified building levees in the Trinity River bottoms and straightening the river, which extended from the mouth of Turtle Creek southward almost four miles. Moving the

Kessler's comprehensive plan addressed eight other actions necessary to beautify the city and stabilize commercial life:

Belt Railroad—Construct a belt railroad which loops around Dallas and Oak Cliff and connects in the Trinity River bottoms to allow track removal and grade

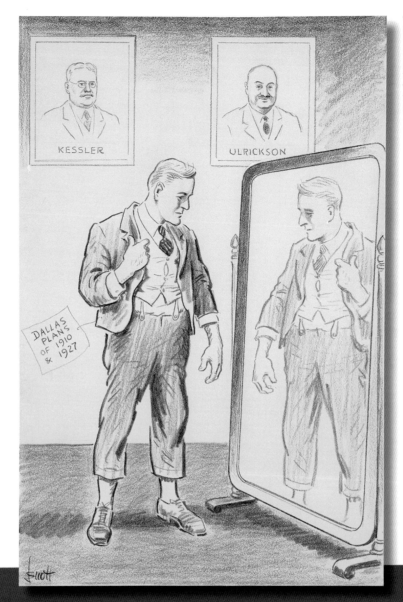

Union Station—Build a union station conveniently located at the western edge of the business district to consolidate five railroad passenger terminals and the connecting railroad tracks of nine railroads.

Freight Terminals—Erect joint freight terminals for local business to better facilitate the handling of freight and eliminate some of the individual freight stations.

Civic Center—Utilize properties near the proposed union station for a civic center and park to provide a beautiful setting to the railroad entrance to Dallas.

Grade Crossings—Eliminate the railroad grade crossings in the downtown district and remove the Texas and Pacific tracks on Pacific Avenue to allow for proper

Street Openings—Widen, open, and realign the streets in the downtown district to relieve congestion and increase property values.

Parks, Parkways, and Boulevards—Build a citywide system of parks, parkways, and connecting boulevards to give all residents the full benefit of outdoor recreation.

Playgrounds—Provide additional playgrounds to accommodate more space for outdoor games, shelters, and playground equipment.

To meet the needs of the rapidly expanding city, Kessler revised his plan in 1919 and 1920. In 1927, the city adopted the Ulrickson Plan, a bond program that addressed some of the still unfinished work recommended by the late

John Knott's cartoon for *The Dallas Morning News* illustrated Dallas residents' support for the triple underpass and park. Courtesy Dallas Historical Society

derpass, Dallas, Texas   DA-4

16451

Built during the fervor of the Texas Centennial, the triple underpass became known as the "Front Door of Dallas." Courtesy Jeff Dunn

The triple underpass...will be one of the most imposing sights in Dallas.

It will be located at the 'front door' of Dallas since it will be the entrance for Highway No. 1 into the city—the most heavily traveled highway in Texas.

The Dallas Morning News, August 20, 1935

Although not part of the Kessler Plan, a significant planning solution came in the 1930s— a triple underpass. Constructed over Bryan's original town site, on land donated by G.B. Dealey, this major new gateway gave easy access to downtown Dallas and alleviated traffic problems. After razing buildings, engineers restructured three primary streets—Elm to the north, Main in the center, and Commerce to the south—to slope down to the west and merge into one. This thoroughfare passes under a railroad bridge between Union Station two blocks to the south and a railroad switching tower one block to the north. Known as the "triple underpass," this triangular design is a civic accomplishment of engineering genius. The arched gateway, constructed of concrete with distinctive Art Deco-style detailing, opened to wide acclaim and created a commanding entrance to the city from the west and an impressive exit from the east. During the excitement of the 1936 Texas Centennial, G.B. Dealey officially dedicated the triple underpass by riding in the first car that passed through it.

Brochures, such as this one, advertised the Texas Centennial Celebration and established Dallas as the leading city in the state. The Sixth Floor Museum at Dealy Plaza.

I'm not here to talk about the past, I'm here to talk about the future. The future is Dallas, Texas.

ROBERT L. THORNTON, banker, city leader, and future mayor of Dallas to the members of the Centennial Commission, 1935

Centennial Fervor: The Making of Big D

In 1935, Robert "R.L." Thornton, then president of Mercantile National Bank, knew the Texas Centennial Exposition would be one of the most important events in Texas and launched a vigorous campaign to host the celebration. "From a cold blooded dollars and cents view, this exposition will mean more to Dallas than anything else," argued Thornton. Represented by Thornton, Dallas outbid

George Dahl of the Dallas firm of Green, La Roche & Dahl was selected as chief architect and technical director of the $25 million project in Fair Park, the home of the Texas State Fair since 1886. Twenty-one of the 50 buildings that Dahl designed in the modern style, later known as Art Deco, were permanent. They spread across a site the size of a small town.

The Texas State Fairgrounds in Dallas showcased the Texas Centennial Exposition in 1936. Courtesy Texas/Dallas History and Archives Division, Dallas Public Library

Made by the Meyer Boot Company, Houston, Texas, these cowboy boots were a gift to A.L. "Red" Vollmann from Colonel W.T. Johnson. Col. Johnson organized the World Championship Rodeo and Vollmann was in charge of special events for the Centennial. Courtesy Dallas Historical Society

With the theme of Texas' progress and romantic history, the exposition opened on June 6, 1936, in Dallas. Six days later, President Roosevelt visited the fairgrounds and declared the centennial was not just for Texans but also for all people in the nation.

Eight months later, when the centennial proved to be a huge triumph and the economic benefits were enormous, Dallas became known as "Big D," a fitting nickname for the recognized and rapidly-growing cosmopolitan city.

Historian Kenneth Ragsdale credited the 1936 Texas Centennial and its broad spectrum of experiences—social, cultural, and economic—for changing the image of Dallas.

Dealey's Park

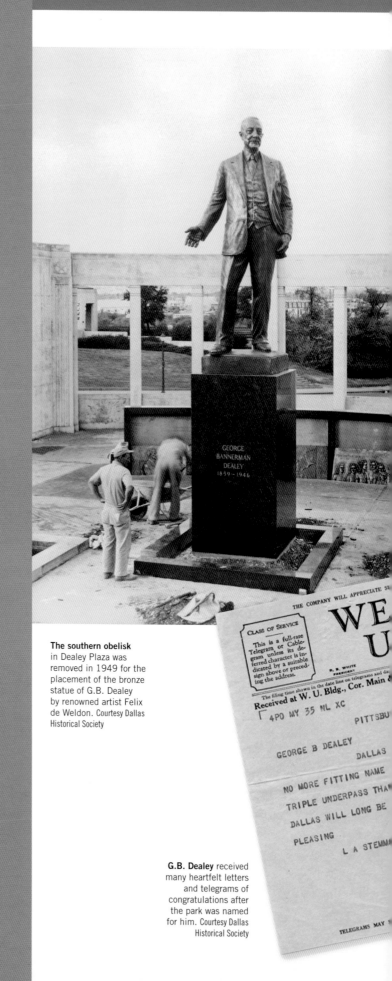

After the triple underpass was built, the remaining land between the streets and to the north of Elm and the south of Commerce, irregular in shape and undesirable for private ownership, was transferred to the Park Board for development as a public park. In 1935, the proposed park was called Dealey Plaza to honor Dallas civic leader G.B. Dealey for his longtime efforts to better the city.

The Dealey Plaza beautification project, which spanned five years, was a cooperative effort of the City of Dallas, the Texas Highway Department, and the Works Progress Administration (WPA). In 1937, the Park Board transferred the project to the National Youth Administration (NYA), a branch of the WPA. Kansas City architects Hare & Hare designed the landscaping and Art Deco-styled structures in Dealey Plaza to complement the details on the triple underpass. Completed in 1941, the Plaza and the adjacent triple underpass became well known as the "Front Door of Dallas."

Three years after G.B. Dealey's death in 1946, the Park Board installed a statue of him in the park. The bronze figure, sculpted by Felix de Weldon, was unveiled and dedicated in Dealey Plaza on November 14, 1949.

During the 1950s and 1960s, Dealey Plaza remained not only the historic birthplace of the city, but the vehicular park also continued to serve as an attractive thoroughfare for traffic entering and leaving the downtown district.

The southern obelisk in Dealey Plaza was removed in 1949 for the placement of the bronze statue of G.B. Dealey by renowned artist Felix de Weldon. Courtesy Dallas Historical Society

G.B. Dealey received many heartfelt letters and telegrams of congratulations after the park was named for him. Courtesy Dallas Historical Society

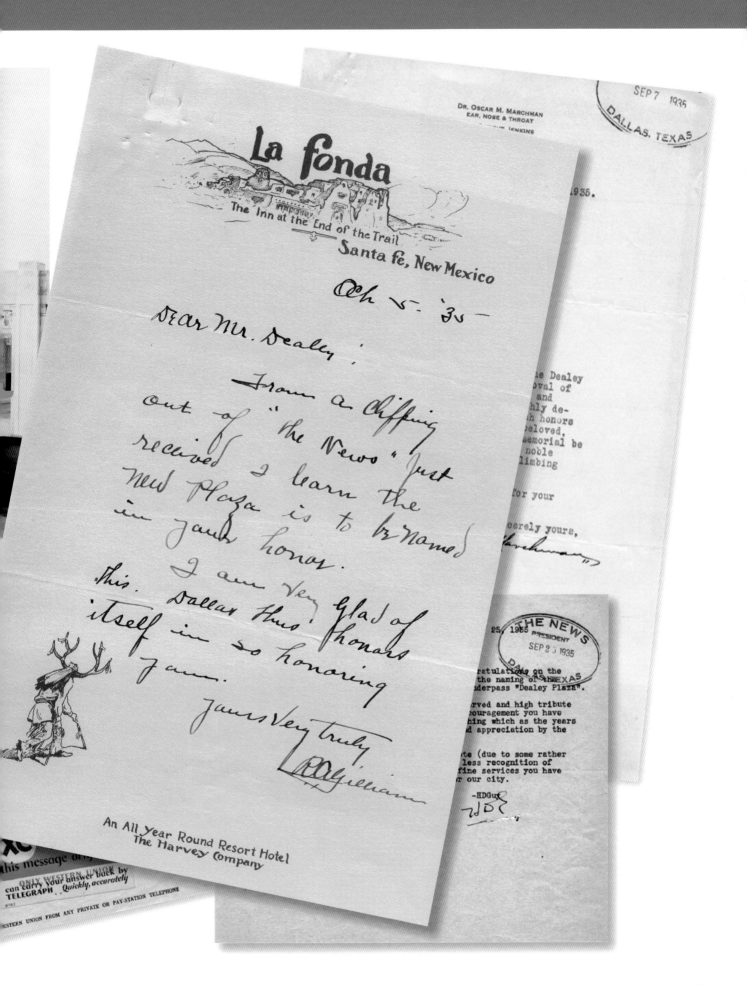

La fonda

The Inn at the End of the Trail

Santa Fe, New Mexico

Oct 5 '35 —

Dear Mr. Dealey;

From a clipping out of "The News" just received I learn the new plaza is to be named in your honor.

I am very glad of this. Dallas thus honors itself in so honoring you.

Yours very truly,
G. B. Dealey

NYA workers made bricks for the streets of La Villita in 1939. Courtesy UT Institute of Texan Cultures at San Antonio

A SECT ON OF ROSE GARDEN, ROCK SPRINGS PARK FORT WORTH, TEXAS—52

The Botanic Garden in Fort Worth was a project of Roosevelt's New Deal. The Sixth Floor Museum at Dealey Plaza

Roosevelt's New Deal

The Great Depression's hardships inspired many public works programs for the unemployed as part of President Franklin D. Roosevelt's New Deal Program. The Works Progress Administration (WPA) was established in 1935. The National Youth Administration (NYA), a branch of the WPA and brainchild of First Lady Eleanor Roosevelt, provided part-time work for unemployed youths. Park development and construction were a popular means of relief supported by these programs. The restored La Villita in downtown San Antonio, the Fort Worth Botanic Garden, and Dealey Plaza are results of New Deal projects in Texas.

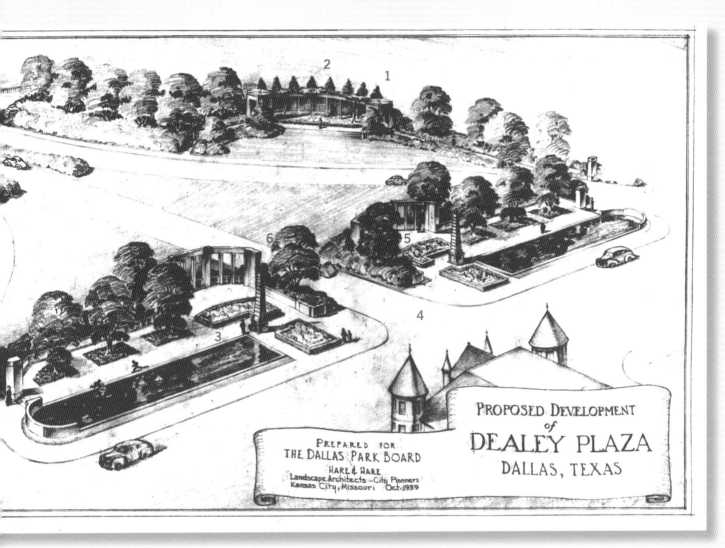

Architects Hare and Hare envisioned Dealey Plaza, a three-acre vehicular park, as the major gateway to the City of Dallas. Courtesy Dallas Historical Society

Park Structures and Plantings

The placement of the Art Deco-style structures is classically symmetrical.

1 At the north and south boundaries of the park, broad steps lead to concrete pergolas.

2 Arched colonnades, flanked on either end by a covered shelter, define the pergolas.

3 Long twin reflecting pools with fountains run north-south along the west side of Houston Street.

4 The reflecting pools are separated by Main Street.

5 Planter boxes and peristyles complement the reflecting pools.

6 One of two tall concrete obelisks was replaced in 1949 with the statue of G.B. Dealey.

Original plantings included live oak, yaupon and cedar trees, Chinese privets, gold flame honeysuckles, big leaf periwinkles, and Chinese wisteria. In 1961, beds of red and white azaleas with dwarf yaupon holly were designed for the planter boxes.

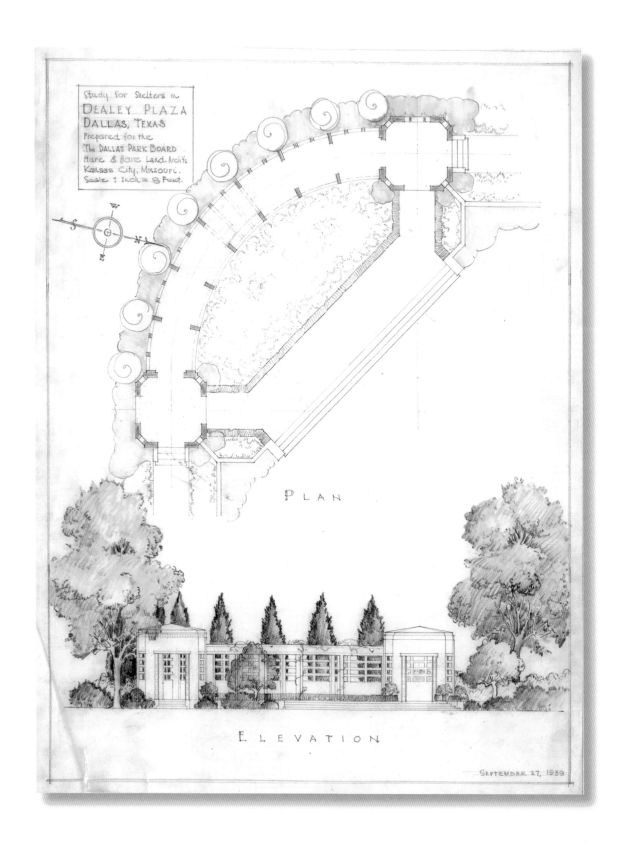

Study for Shelters in
DEALEY PLAZA
DALLAS, TEXAS
Prepared for the
The DALLAS PARK BOARD
Hare & Hare Land. Arch'ts
Kansas City, Missouri.
Scale 1 Inch = 8 Feet.

PLAN

ELEVATION

September 27, 1939

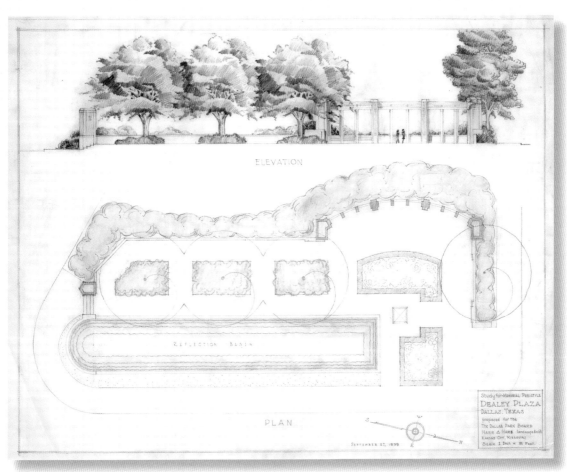

ELEVATION

PLAN

REFLECTION BASIN

Study for Memorial Peristyle
DEALEY PLAZA
DALLAS, TEXAS
prepared for the
THE DALLAS PARK BOARD
HARE & HARE landscape arch.
KANSAS CITY, MISSOURI
SCALE 1 INCH = 20 FEET

SEPTEMBER 27, 1939

Architects Hare and Hare
submitted these plans
for shelters and peristyles
to the Park Board on
September 27, 1939.
Courtesy Dallas Historical Society

*We were categorized as a City of Hate...
I dislike that phrase a lot because
City of Hate was not only **not** descriptive
of what we were, it was descriptive
of the very thing we were **not**.*

J. ERIK JONSSON, civic leader and former mayor of Dallas,
Oral History Project, The Sixth Floor Museum at Dealey
Plaza, August 17, 1992

The Dallas Morning
News that announced
Kennedy's assassination
was printed by this plate.
(Plate): Courtesy A.H. Belo
Corporation Collection/The
Sixth Floor Museum at Dealey
Plaza; (Newspaper): Phil Willis
Collection/The Sixth Floor
Museum at Dealey Plaza

Frame 23 of the Orville
Nix home movie shows
the effects of the fatal
shot. Nix Collection/The Sixth
Floor Museum at Dealey Plaza

When President John F. Kennedy was assassinated in Dealey Plaza on November 22, 1963, Dallas' pride in her civic center was in jeopardy. The proud cradle of the city's history suddenly became a murder site recognized throughout the world. Public opinion polls, conducted shortly after the assassination, indicated over 80% of Americans had indicted "the people of Dallas" for the crime. Eighty-six percent of the locals reported feeling shame that the event happened here. Joe M. Dealey, grandson of the community builder, expressed his heartfelt reaction to a reporter, "We are a tormented town." A state judge added, "...the eyes of the world are upon us— and they will be looking with a critical stare."

After the assassination, Dallas residents were harassed—telephone operators disconnected long-distance calls and restaurants refused service. In Pennsylvania, a gas station attendant threw a fistful of coins in a Texas driver's face. In Detroit, a Dallas man was ejected from a cab, and in Europe, foreigners exclaimed when introduced to a Dallas history professor, "Oh you're from Dallas? That's where they kill presidents."

Please Forgive Us

T he day after the assassination, Dallas citizens began to bring flowers and mementos to Dealey Plaza. Pinned on a spray of carnations, a card apologized:

We love You-

Please Forgive us-

The Ted Wilson Family

"God forgive us all," begged another. A nine-year-old Dallas girl wrote in red crayon: "I'm sorry Caroline and John John. Forgive us."

Thousands of people passed these makeshift shrines; guards watched over the site. These were the first acts to transform Dealey Plaza into a memorial to honor the slain President.

...when I got there, the whole place was covered with wreaths and cards and flowers. I was amazed. The knoll was covered with these wreaths, floral designs, and... I walked through this field of memories and read them...

it was a very emotional, kind of wonderful, sad peace.

IKE PAPPAS, former WNEW New York radio reporter, Oral History Project, The Sixth Floor Museum at Dealey Plaza, March 1, 1993

By November 23, large makeshift memorials for Kennedy had been assembled in Dealey Plaza. Robert Russell Collection/The Sixth Floor Museum at Dealey Plaza

The idea of a sacred place, like an empty tomb,
struck me as something fitting
as long as it was abstract...

It was essential to me that whatever I did, it should only be tacit interpretation of a memorial per se;
it would be left to the viewers to find their own meaning.

PHILIP JOHNSON, architect, reflecting on his design
for the Kennedy Memorial

The John F. Kennedy Memorial, designed by Philip Johnson, was dedicated at a site two blocks east of Dealey Plaza in 1970. Steven Watson/The Sixth Floor Museum at Dealey Plaza

A Fitting Tribute

The decent thing to do is let some time elapse.

J. ERIK JONSSON, civic leader and future mayor of Dallas, November 1963

Visitors gathered in Dealey Plaza on November 22, 2001, to pay homage to President Kennedy. The Sixth Floor Museum at Dealey Plaza

After the assassination, seven years passed before the Dallas community finally dedicated a memorial to President John F. Kennedy—but it was not in Dealey Plaza or the former Texas School Book Depository building. The monument, designed by Philip Johnson as a cenotaph—an open, empty tomb—was erected two blocks east of the assassination site in a new park called John F. Kennedy Memorial Plaza. A dedication ceremony was held on June 24, 1970.

It was the millions of visitors, not the community, who turned Dealey Plaza into a site of commemoration. After the tragedy, the park offered pedestrians a dramatic setting for quiet reflection.

For about twenty years, semi-formal ceremonies marked the anniversary of the assassination in Dealey Plaza. After 1983, the city and county honored the Kennedy family's request to encourage citizens to celebrate the President's birthday on May 29, rather than his death. Still, people spontaneously gather in Dealey Plaza every year on November 22.

Reconciliation

There were some in Dallas who wanted to tear down the Texas School Book Depository building. After community debate, Dallas County acquired the building in 1977 with plans to locate county offices on the first through fifth floors. Because evidence was found and investigations concluded that shots were fired from a window on the building's sixth floor, that floor was preserved. Beginning in 1977, the Dallas County Historical Commission initiated a plan to interpret the site. As plans progressed, the Dallas County Historical Foundation was incorporated in 1983 to oversee the completion of the project. In 1989, the Sixth Floor Exhibit opened to the public to help visitors find meaning in the tragic event.

Three decades after the assassination, in October 1993, the Secretary of the Interior designated Dealey Plaza a National Historic Landmark District. This new historic status acknowledged that the spot where John F. Kennedy died was an important part of United States history.

Official dedication ceremonies were held on November 22, 1993, the thirtieth anniversary of Kennedy's death. Thousands gathered at the site. Nellie Connally dedicated the bronze landmark plaque "to future generations of Americans, with the hope that the legacy of John F. Kennedy will inspire them to reach for greatness in their own lives." Since then, Dealey Plaza has become a new source of pride for the city and serves just as G.B. Dealey envisioned it—as the "Front Door of Dallas."

The Sixth Floor Museum exhibits, with 350 photographs and six videos, as well as original artifacts, chronicles the assassination and legacy of John F. Kennedy. The Sixth Floor Museum at Dealey Plaza

Step into Dealey Plaza, and you feel you are on sacred ground... This is the necessary pilgrimage.

JOHN McADAMS, Ph.D., professor of political science, Marquette University, Milwaukee, Wisconsin, from his Web site, 1995-2002

46

The National Historic Landmark District was officially dedicated on the thirtieth anniversary of the assassination in 1993. Thousands of Dallasites attended the event. Ronald D. Rice/The Sixth Floor Museum at Dealey Plaza

The sniper's perch was faithfully recreated as part of the educational exhibits at The Sixth Floor Museum at Dealey Plaza. The Sixth Floor Museum at Dealey Plaza

In **1991,** Oliver Stone recreated Dealey Plaza to its 1963 appearance for his conspiracy film, *JFK*. Courtesy David Woo/*The Dallas Morning News.*

Oliver Stone's *JFK*

Dealey Plaza and the assassination story again took headlines in 1991 when Hollywood producer Oliver Stone brought his crew to Dallas to film *JFK,* starring Kevin Costner. *JFK* was Stone's personal interpretation of a conspiracy to kill Kennedy and focused on New Orleans District Attorney Jim Garrison's probe into the assassination. For the filming, Hollywood prop masters restored much of Dealey Plaza to its 1963 appearance. Restoration included painting and constructing facades on the former Texas School Book Depository building, fabricating railroad tracks, pruning trees and bushes to their 1963 size, and mounting 1963-style traffic signs at their original locations. This event brought renewed interest to the site for many local people; some even served as extras.

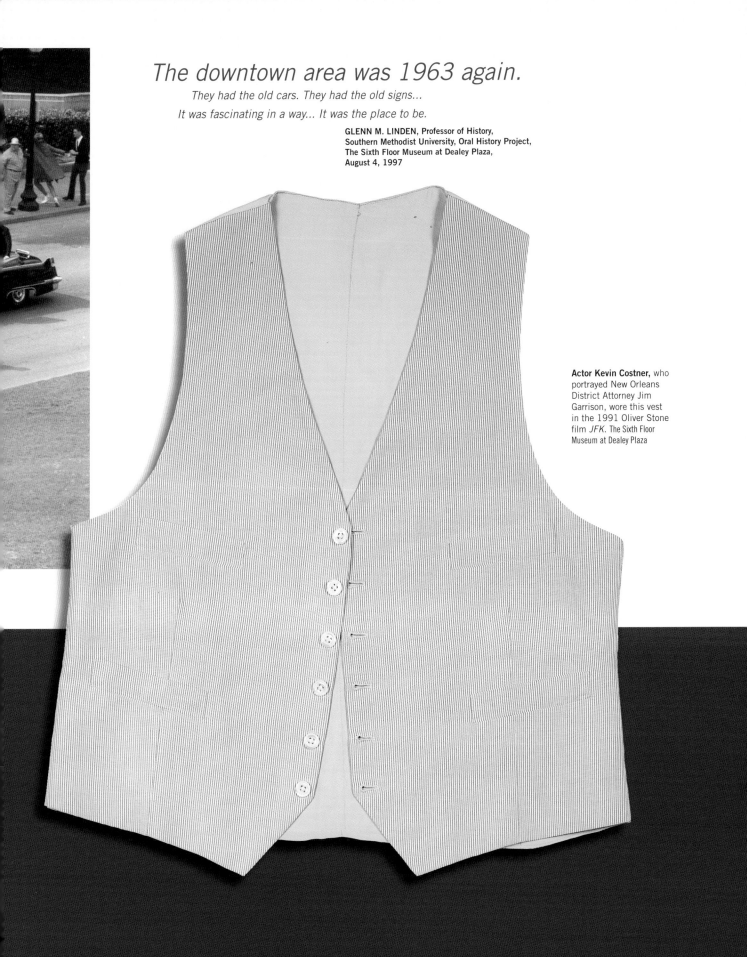

The downtown area was 1963 again.

They had the old cars. They had the old signs...

It was fascinating in a way... It was the place to be.

GLENN M. LINDEN, Professor of History,
Southern Methodist University, Oral History Project,
The Sixth Floor Museum at Dealey Plaza,
August 4, 1997

Actor Kevin Costner, who
portrayed New Orleans
District Attorney Jim
Garrison, wore this vest
in the 1991 Oliver Stone
film *JFK*. The Sixth Floor
Museum at Dealey Plaza

The Restoration Project

The Sixth Floor Museum at Dealey Plaza recently proposed restoring Dealey Plaza to its 1963 historic integrity. Working with a task force of dedicated individuals representing the City of Dallas Park and Recreation Department, the Dallas Park Board, the Downtown Improvement District, and The Belo Foundation, the Museum summarized and recorded historical research on the Plaza. The consultant team of MESA Design Group and Good Fulton & Farrell developed a master plan documenting the specific restoration needs and associated costs. The plan addresses the historic site in context of architectural and structural conditions, fountain restoration and repair, hardscape conditions and handicap access (ADA), lighting, landscape, irrigation, utilities, and graphic signage.

Approximately $3,000,000 is currently being sought to fund the restoration.

...the [Kennedy] tragedy is a part of our city's history and...
the fact that it occurred here in modern times
[is] going to bring people to Dealey Plaza...

ROBERT DECHERD, Chairman, President, and CEO
of Belo Corp., Oral History Project, The Sixth Floor
Museum at Dealey Plaza, March 2, 2001

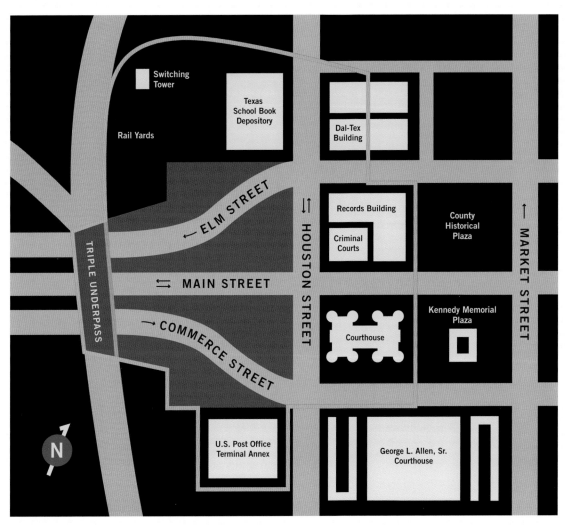

Switching Tower

Texas School Book Depository

Rail Yards

Dal-Tex Building

Records Building

County Historical Plaza

Criminal Courts

ELM STREET

HOUSTON STREET

MAIN STREET

TRIPLE UNDERPASS

COMMERCE STREET

Courthouse

Kennedy Memorial Plaza

MARKET STREET

N

U.S. Post Office Terminal Annex

George L. Allen, Sr. Courthouse

This map shows the area included in the Dealey Plaza National Historic Landmark District outlined in gold. Dealey Plaza and the triple underpass, which The Sixth Floor Museum at Dealey Plaza proposes for restoration, are noted in red. The Sixth Floor Museum at Dealey Plaza

Opposite page: The structures, hardscape, and landscape elements in Dealey Plaza have deteriorated and many elements have been modified over the years. The Sixth Floor Museum at Dealey Plaza

Based on the detailed analysis of the historical research and the physical investigation of the structures and property, the planning team made the following recommendations for restoration.

★ **Architecture**—The Art Deco-style architectural structures—pergolas, shelters, colonnades, peristyles, and planter boxes—will undergo major cleaning with manual and power solution blast methods. The concrete will be repaired as necessary, then primed and painted to match the existing finish. All lead-based paint will be removed and surfaces will be repainted with lead-free paint.

★ **Fountains**—Three additional fountains with a four-foot spray jet at either end will be installed in each reflecting pool to achieve the original design intent and the 1963 condition. New coping, basin filtration, pumps, piping, waterproofing, water treatment, lighting, and nozzles will ensure efficient operation.

★ **Lighting**—To achieve consistency throughout the Plaza, existing street lighting will be replaced with luminaries, and new light poles will be designed and painted to match their 1963 appearance. The triple underpass bridge will be lighted using the existing foundations present at the base of the underpass columns. New lighting will be installed in the peristyles and at the columns at the end of the planter walls.

★ **Hardscape and ADA**—Paving in the Plaza will be demolished and replaced with paving of uniform color featuring a scored pattern similar to that present in 1963. Brick planter walls beneath the live oak trees will be removed to ensure the health and vitality of the trees. The brick walls will be replaced with custom-made, decorative landscape iron wickets similar to those currently used throughout the Plaza.

Curbs and gutters will be replaced to accommodate curb cuts and handicap ramps. Crosswalks will be repaved and repainted with updated markings and protective striping. The curb at the southeast corner of Commerce and Houston Streets will be extended to more easily accommodate pedestrian traffic.

★ **Landscape**—Dead or dying trees will be removed and replaced with appropriate healthy ones. To replicate the 1963 landscape design, dwarf yaupon, copperleaf, and a bed of lantana will be added. All groundcover and barren flowerbeds will be replanted to provide a more verdant landscape conducive to shade.

★ **Irrigation**—All broken sprinkler heads will be replaced. Pop-up spray heads will be raised or lowered accordingly to achieve maximum coverage and unobstructed distribution of water. Plastic nozzles will be replaced with brass nozzles so that the system continues the correct precipitation and distribution as that in the original design. Diagnostic tests will be conducted on the remote control valves and existing water meters.

★ **Utilities**—Exposed gas lines will be relocated underground or in landscape zones. Likewise, meter boxes will be moved out of public view and utility boxes located on traffic signs will be buried underground. The power transformer for the fountains will be replaced if necessary.

★ **Graphic Signage**—Existing signage, including the WPA, NYA, and the National Historic Landmark District markers, will be cleaned and polished to improve their worn appearance. A new pedestrian wayfinding system, incorporating the historic markers and existing general information, will guide visitors from The Sixth Floor Museum at Dealey Plaza, through Dealey Plaza, and to the John F. Kennedy Memorial Plaza.

Restoration Project Task Force

The Sixth Floor Museum at Dealey Plaza

Jeff West

Karen Wiley

Bob Canavan

Ruth Ann Rugg

Lacie Ballinger

Arlinda Abbott

Dallas Park and Recreation Department

Rob Parks

Willis Winters

John Reynolds

Renee Otote

Reginald Hurd

Downtown Improvement District

Patty Kleinknecht

The Belo Foundation

Judith Segura

MESA Design Group

Tary Arterburn

Bill Millsap

Sandra Bolain

Paul Freeland

Alisha Hughes

Good Fulton and Farrell

Larry Good

Nestor Zabala

For additional information about the Sixth Floor Museum's exhibitions, publications, Oral History Program, or for contributions, please contact:

The Sixth Floor Museum at Dealey Plaza

411 Elm Street, Suite 120

Dallas, Texas 75202-3301

214 747-6660

214 747-6662 Fax

www.jfk.org

Dealey Plaza, shown here in 1955, was a vehicular park in 1963 when President Kennedy was assassinated. Courtesy Texas/ Dallas History and Archives Division, Dallas Public Library